MW00785992

World War II Women in Uniform

Martha Sias Purcell

Perfection Learning®

Dedication

This book is dedicated to Zoe Jordan, Cheryl Cocking, Pauline Cram, and Betty Decatur. These special ladies served in the WAVES during World War II.

Special recognition goes to Colonel Louis D. Erbstein, Curator of the Fort Des Moines Museum. He is dedicated to the preservation of this history, which began at Fort Des Moines in 1942 with 440 WAACs.

Editorial Director: Susan C. Thies
Editor: Mary L. Bush

Cover Design: Michael A. Aspengren
Book Design: Jill M. Kline, Deborah Lea Bell
Image Research: Lisa Lorimor

IMAGE CREDITS
©CORBIS: pp. 4, 18, 20, 21, 23 (bottom), 30, 31 (bottom)

ArtToday(www.arttoday.com): pp. 8, 27; ©Digital Stock: pp. 2–3, 4–5 (bkgd), 6, 7, 8–9, 12–13 (bkgd), 17 (bkgd), 24–25, 28–29 (bkgd), 32–33 (bkgd), 39, 40, 43, 44 (top); Franklin D. Roosevelt Library: pp. 12–13 (bottom), 35 (bottom), 36, 38; Jill M. Kline: 37; Library of Congress: pp. 5, 10, 19, 32; National Archives: pp. 1, 11, 13, 14, 15, 16, 17, 23 (top), 26, 28, 31 (top), 33, 34, 35 (top), 44 (bottom)

For information, contact
Perfection Learning® Corporation
1000 North Second Avenue, P.O. Box 500
Logan, Iowa 51546-0500.
Phone: 1-800-831-4190 • Fax: 1-800-543-2745
perfectionlearning.com

1 2 3 4 5 BA 06 05 04 03 02

Paperback ISBN 0-7891-5904-x

Contents

Jesse Owens makes the long jump that set an Olympic record at the 1936 Games.

INTRODUCTION

THE 1936 Olympic Games were held in Berlin, Germany. Adolf Hitler, Germany's leader, watched with pride. The Olympics would show everyone that Germany and its people were **superior**.

Then Jesse Owens, an African American man from the United States, won his fourth gold medal. Disgusted, Hitler left the stands. He'd find another way to show the world.

Years before, Hitler had written *Mein Kampf (My Struggle)*. This book detailed his plan to conquer the world and rule it with a **master race** of people. The late 1930s was the perfect time to accomplish this goal.

Disagreements caused by the end of World War I still threatened Europe. The **Great Depression** had just swept through the world, and people were worried about money and jobs. A **dictator** could easily gain a loyal following by promising to bring a country back to greatness.

Adolf Hitler

5

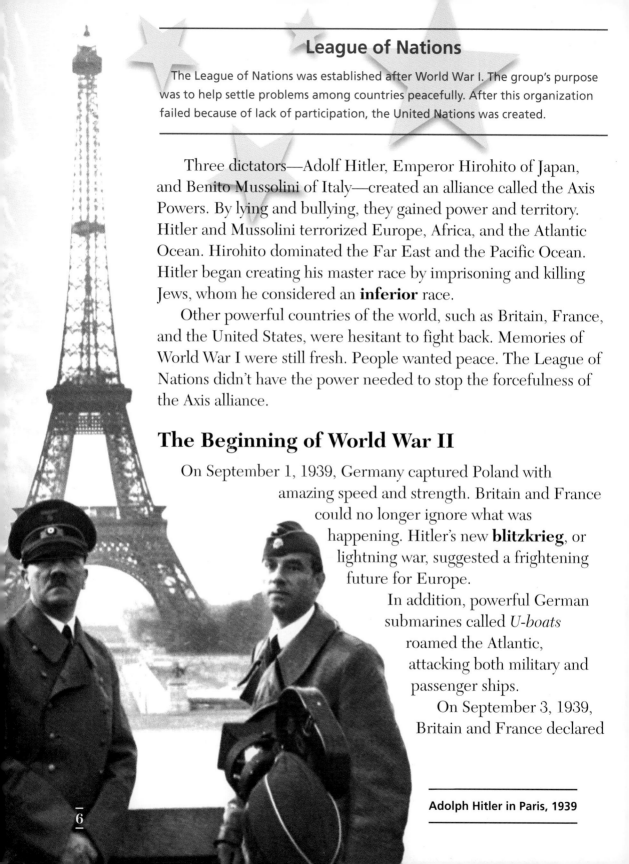

League of Nations

The League of Nations was established after World War I. The group's purpose was to help settle problems among countries peacefully. After this organization failed because of lack of participation, the United Nations was created.

Three dictators—Adolf Hitler, Emperor Hirohito of Japan, and Benito Mussolini of Italy—created an alliance called the Axis Powers. By lying and bullying, they gained power and territory. Hitler and Mussolini terrorized Europe, Africa, and the Atlantic Ocean. Hirohito dominated the Far East and the Pacific Ocean. Hitler began creating his master race by imprisoning and killing Jews, whom he considered an **inferior** race.

Other powerful countries of the world, such as Britain, France, and the United States, were hesitant to fight back. Memories of World War I were still fresh. People wanted peace. The League of Nations didn't have the power needed to stop the forcefulness of the Axis alliance.

The Beginning of World War II

On September 1, 1939, Germany captured Poland with amazing speed and strength. Britain and France could no longer ignore what was happening. Hitler's new **blitzkrieg**, or lightning war, suggested a frightening future for Europe.

In addition, powerful German submarines called *U-boats* roamed the Atlantic, attacking both military and passenger ships.

On September 3, 1939, Britain and France declared

Adolph Hitler in Paris, 1939

war on Germany. They led the Allies, the nations opposing the Axis countries. World War II had begun.

Germany conquered France, but Britain continued to fight. London, Britain's capital, suffered nightly bombings, but the British Royal Air Force continued to return fire. Italy and Germany worked together to maintain control of North Africa.

The United States Enters the War

When the war began, people in the United States felt safe. The Atlantic and Pacific Oceans separated them from any **combat**.

However, on December 7, 1941, Japan surprised the U.S. naval base at Pearl Harbor with a crushing air attack. A few hours later, Japan began raids on U.S. military bases in the Philippine Islands.

The United States entered World War II when Congress and President Franklin Roosevelt declared war on Japan on December 8, 1941.

Attack on Pearl Harbor, Hawaii, 1941

D-Day

The Allied invasion of Normandy is commonly called D-Day. D-Day is the term given to any secret date for a military operation.

Patriotism was high. Every U.S. citizen became a "soldier" by sacrificing tires, gasoline, and foods needed for the war effort. Families proudly sent their men onto the battlefields to serve their country.

For the next two years, the fighting raged on. Finally, in 1943, the Allies regained control of North Africa. Italy signed a secret peace agreement with the United States and declared war on Germany.

The Invasion of Normandy, France

In an attempt to end the war, U.S. General Dwight D. Eisenhower directed a massive attack on territory held by Germany. The plan involved every military **branch** and **unit** of the Allies. Even though thousands of troops were involved in this invasion, Eisenhower managed an amazing amount of secrecy.

On June 6, 1944, the Allied troops began landing on the beaches of Normandy, France. **Paratroopers** jumped from airplanes over enemy territory. Land, sea, and air battles were fought fiercely by both sides. Thousands of Allied soldiers died, but the invasion of France eventually crippled the Germans.

General Dwight D. Eisenhower

Victory in Europe

The Germans' last major attack was the Battle of the Bulge. This action earned its name because Germany created a bulging battle line across the Belgian countryside. In spite of this, the Allies pushed the German troops back and took control of the area. By January 16, 1945, it was clear that Hitler would lose the war.

Germany surrendered on May 7, 1945, and people celebrated V-E Day (Victory in Europe). Japan was still a problem, but now the Allies could direct all their energies toward the Pacific Ocean.

What Happened to the Leaders?

On April 12, 1945, President Roosevelt suffered a fatal stroke. Some Americans were afraid the Allies would lose the war without him. Vice President Harry S. Truman was sworn in as president and continued to lead the United States to victory.

About three weeks after Roosevelt's death, Hitler committed suicide along with some of his devoted followers. They had been hiding in an underground command center.

American troops on the coast of France, 1944

The city of Hiroshima was destroyed by the atom bomb.

Victory in Japan

After several bloody battles, the United States gradually regained the Pacific islands that had been controlled by Japan. However, the Allies knew the Japanese believed in a fight to the death. They would never give up.

President Truman feared that thousands of Allied lives could be lost in a land invasion of Japan. So he decided to force a sudden surrender instead. The president ordered the first use of an atomic bomb in a war.

On August 6, 1945, the city of Hiroshima, Japan, was leveled by this powerful weapon. The world had never seen such destruction from a single bomb. More than 90,000 people were killed. Almost as many were injured. Thousands more suffered from radiation sickness.

Three days later, Truman was surprised that Emperor Hirohito had still not surrendered. So Truman ordered a second bomb dropped on Nagasaki, Japan.

On August 14, 1945, Japan finally gave up. V-J Day (Victory in Japan) meant that World War II was over.

Free a Man to Fight

For over 200 years, women have taken part in America's wars. Women replaced their injured or dead husbands on the battle lines of the American Revolution. During the Civil War, women disguised themselves as men in order to fight. In World War I, women volunteered for non-combat duty, but they weren't considered official members of the armed forces. They had to supply their own food, housing, and protection while they served.

A Women's Army Auxiliary Corps (WAAC) unit stationed at Fort Des Moines, Iowa

When the United States entered World War II, women wanted an official role in the military. In May 1941, Congresswoman Edith Nourse Rogers presented a bill that would establish a Women's Army Corps. General George C. Marshall, the Army Chief of Staff, agreed that women could play an important role in the military. But other generals and congressmen disagreed. "A woman's place is in the home!" they said. Respectable employment for women was limited to teaching, nursing, or secretarial jobs.

However, the attack on Pearl Harbor made people look at the idea differently. The United States would be fighting a war on two **fronts**—Europe and Japan. There would be shortages of manpower in the military. Women were already well trained in office skills. Why couldn't they put these skills to use in the military? They could free a man from a desk job so he could fight.

Most families supported their daughters' plans to join the military. However, some mothers claimed these women were cheating their sons out of a safe desk job and forcing their boys into battle.

The Women's Army Auxiliary Corps

Army officers believed that if women were allowed to join the military, they should remain **civilians** and not have full military status. They would be given uniforms and training, but not benefits like government life insurance and **veterans** medical coverage. After much compromise, Congress passed a bill that established the Women's Army Auxiliary Corps (WAAC). The bill was signed by President Roosevelt on May 15, 1942.

While this bill made the army the first service to include women, it did not make them equal. It clearly stated that the WAAC was to work *with* the army rather than be *in* the army.

Eleanor Roosevelt and Oveta Culp Hobby

Posters recruited women for military service.

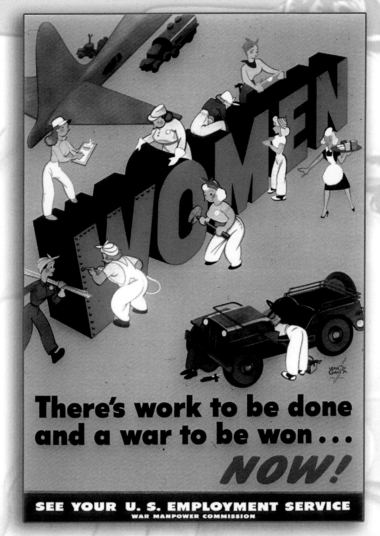

There's work to be done and a war to be won . . .
NOW!

SEE YOUR U. S. EMPLOYMENT SERVICE
WAR MANPOWER COMMISSION

Oveta Culp Hobby was the first director of the WAAC. She faced many battles as she tried to pave the way for women in the military.

The men resented women in their army. Many jokes were made about WAACs. For a while, bitter servicemen started rumors, claiming that WAACs were wild and had low moral character.

Reporters smirked when they asked Hobby silly questions at press conferences. Would the WAACs wear khaki-colored underwear? Would boot camp have special classes in makeup?

Hobby had no decision-making power either. Even her suggestions for the first uniforms were ignored. Instead, the army's quartermaster general designed them. He was the officer in charge of all uniforms for the U.S. Army. Later these uniforms were found to be unsuitable for the military women.

WAACs in Training

The first WAAC training center was at Fort Des Moines in Des Moines, Iowa. The fort had been a **cavalry** post for 40 years. The stables and other buildings had to be transformed into WAAC living quarters.

THIS IS MY WAR TOO!
WOMEN'S ARMY AUXILIARY CORPS
UNITED · STATES · ARMY

Women were eager to join the military for a variety of reasons. Many saw it as their patriotic duty. They wanted to help the war effort in any way they could. A few had lost a loved one and wanted to take his place. Others joined because they were bored with their jobs and wanted to do something exciting and different.

Presidential Post

Former president Ronald Reagan learned to ride horses and became a second lieutenant at Fort Des Moines in 1937.

Two WAACs repairing a military truck

Thousands applied for the first few available positions. WAACs were required to be U.S. citizens, 21–45 years old, at least 5 feet tall, and free of family responsibilities.

On a hot day in August, the women arrived at Fort Des Moines for basic training. The training lasted four to six weeks. The first class of WAACs had 440 women in it. Four hundred of these women were Caucasian, while forty were African American.

The army had always been segregated, so African American WAACs were assigned to their own **platoon**. They had separate housing and other post facilities, such as beauty parlors and officers' clubs. However, classes were integrated.

Until the first WAAC class of women officers graduated, all training was done by male army officers. Most of these men thought it was beneath them to work with women. Several were obvious about their feelings and treated the women with disrespect.

Women in Other Branches of the Military

Soon other branches of the military decided to **recruit** women too. On July 30, 1942, the WAVES (Women Accepted for Volunteer Emergency Service) became part of the navy. The WAVES were barred from combat, but they were granted full military status like the men.

Mildred McAfee was appointed director of the WAVES. Unlike Oveta Culp Hobby, McAfee had input into decisions. For example, the WAVES uniform was designed by Mainbocher, a well-known fashion designer of the time.

The Marine Corps and the Coast Guard also added women to their organizations with full military status. The Coast Guard women, or SPARs, were created in November 1942. Their name came from the Coast Guard motto *Semper Paratus*, meaning "Always Ready." The SPAR program adopted many of the practices started by the WAVES, including similar uniforms and training.

Fashion in the Military

Main Rousseau Bocher was an American fashion designer known as Mainbocher. He introduced the strapless evening gown and was known for designs including pearl chokers and short white gloves. Mainbocher designed the uniforms for both navy and Coast Guard women.

"THE GIRL OF THE YEAR IS A SPAR"

ENLIST IN THE
COAST GUARD SPARS

APPLY NEAREST COAST GUARD OFFICE

The Marine Corps did not want a nickname for their women. So the "women marines" was established in February 1943.

The success of the WAVES, SPARs, and women marines eliminated possible recruits for the WAAC, so the army was under pressure to change. On July 1, 1943, the WAACs were changed from civilian status to full military status. They became the Women's Army Corps (WAC). Now the WAC was *in* the army.

Boot Camp

A group of young women stood before a uniformed officer. They pledged to serve their country "for the duration plus six months," or until six months after the war was over.

The women had been interviewed by the recruiting officer to discuss their interests and goals. They had passed the physical exam and an aptitude test to determine their abilities. Their new adventure was about to begin.

After they took the oath, the women boarded the troop train that delivered them to boot camp for basic training. Hugs, tears, and sometimes the local high school band bid them farewell.

Troop Trains

Troop trains taught the women their first two lessons of military life. The first was to get used to living with strangers in crowded, no-frills conditions. The second was to learn to wait in line.

Troop trains often traveled across the United States from California to New York. Sleeping cots were jammed into stuffy train cars. Open windows were the only relief from the sweltering mid-summer day.

The Moffat Tunnel was a six-mile-long mountain tunnel in Colorado that provided extra "excitement." When the train entered the tunnel, the girls were too busy laughing and chattering to notice. Smoke and cinders continued to gush from the locomotive's smokestack but had nowhere to go except into the open train windows. Glowing sparks and soot settled on the women, their sheets, and their open suitcases. A few days later, the recruits arrived in New York City still trying to figure out how to remove the scorched and filthy reminders of the Moffat Tunnel.

Boot Camp

If asked to describe a typical day at boot camp, recruits answered with the words *hurried, marching*, and *inspection*.

They hurried to an early breakfast. They hurried to **muster**, to **roll call**, to classes, and to marching practice.

The women marched everywhere—to classes, lunch, dinner, study hours, and their living **quarters** at the end of each exhausting day.

An officer inspected those quarters at least once a week. **Demerits** were given for lint on uniforms, shoes that didn't gleam, and cots with even the slightest wrinkle on top.

Vaccinations were given at boot camp. Recruits moaned when the announcement appeared on the bulletin board. They'd heard about those extra long needles and the recruits who'd fainted.

Every day, the women practiced **close order drill**. Each platoon was expected to march in a single motion, rather than in a jagged line of individual movements.

"Hup, two, three, four," the drill instructor would bark. "Right face" meant turn to the right. "Left face" meant turn to the left. When the recruits became more accomplished, they sang out the rhythm in lively songs.

Military women took pride in their ability to march. Soon competitions developed among platoons. As the women marched and sang, their spirits soared, along with their pride in belonging to an impressive group of people.

Every women's service branch had some of the same basic classes. In addition to drill practice, the women attended physical education. They studied regulations, customs, and courtesies, like who and when to salute. They also learned the **nomenclature**, or vocabulary, used in their branch of the military.

Women in Uniform

For about the first two weeks of boot camp, recruits wore their civilian clothes. The day they received their uniforms was one of excitement and pride.

The women lined up at tables. At one table, they received their first military paychecks, of which $200 went for clothing. At a second table, they collected their uniforms. At a third table, they paid for their uniforms—which took almost all of their paychecks.

Military Money

Military paychecks could be saved, sent home to families, or used to buy supplies. Supplies were available at the PX, or military store.

Members of the WAC model new uniforms.

Women in the military were usually issued a suit. They were also given a hat, a raincoat, a waterproof covering for the hat, a blouse, and a tie. Nylon was used for parachutes, so women wore cotton hose, or stockings, on their legs and feet.

There were no pants in the women's early uniforms or work clothes. But as the war went on and women were given a wider variety of jobs, the uniforms had to change. Activities like repairing airplane engines or tramping through jungles were better achieved in something other than a skirt.

Recruits had mixed feelings the day they packed their civilian clothes to send home. When a military woman looked in the mirror, a smartly uniformed woman smiled back at her. But the box of dresses and open-toed shoes represented the last link to the life she had known before.

Nylon Knowledge

Nylon is a human-made fiber, or thread, invented in the 1930s. Because nylon is strong and stretchy, women's stockings made from this material soon became popular. Other clothing items, such as jogging suits, swimwear, and shorts are also made of nylon. Military items made from nylon include parachutes, protective vests, combat uniforms, and netting.

She's in the Army Now

The WAC paved the way for the rest of her "sister" branches in the U.S. Armed Forces. As the first leader of the WAC, Oveta Culp Hobby found public opinion was one of her greatest problems.

"Women in the military? Never!" some people said. "Who will do the mending and prepare the meals? Why don't they just stay home where they belong?"

But the women of the WAC were determined to prove that the army *was* where they belonged.

Fort Des Moines

Modifying Fort Des Moines from a cavalry post to a women's boot camp was a major undertaking. In the beginning, four hotels in downtown Des Moines were used for housing and classes.

The streets were filled with platoons of WACs marching from one class to another. Cars were scarce anyway because of rubber and gasoline shortages.

Along with the usual classes in boot camp, WACs also had **field training** to prepare them for possible combat situations. The women were instructed in the use of weapons. They also learned how to set up a tent under a variety of circumstances.

The enemy sometimes used deadly gases as weapons. For gas mask training, recruits filed through a chamber filled with dangerous fumes.

The first graduates of Fort Des Moines established new basic training centers at four other army bases in the United States. These new bases were located at Daytona Beach, Florida; Fort Oglethorpe, Georgia; Fort Devens, Massachusetts; and Camp Ruston, Louisiana.

A recruit loads antiaircraft casings into a furnace to mold them for use.

Military women training on a net obstacle

Training for Military Jobs

Following boot camp, WACs were sent to special schools to be trained for their military assignments. At first they served only in secretarial and record-keeping positions. But as the army recognized how skillful women could be, the list of job opportunities grew.

Throughout the war, the WAC trained women as drivers, weather observers and forecasters, **cryptographers**, mechanics, radio operators, sheet metal workers, laboratory and X-ray technicians, parachute **riggers**, photographers, and control tower operators. They also operated statistical-control tabulating machines, which were early versions of today's computers.

WACs also worked as mail censors. Censors blacked out any important military information found in personal mail that might get into the hands of the enemy. The women seemed to have an instinct for spotting phrases a soldier might write to let his wife know where he was.

Some WACs were trusted to work on the Manhattan Project. This was the code name for the secret development of the atomic bomb.

Overseas Assignments

For most of the war, the army was the only branch of the service to send women overseas.

General Eisenhower was hesitant to have women at his headquarters in Algiers, France, until he saw how valuable the British women's units were. Just days after the invasion of North Africa, Eisenhower requested five WAC officers, especially those who spoke French.

Unfortunately, the WACs' ship was torpedoed on the way to this assignment. The rescue at sea involved several days in a life raft for some. All of the women eventually reported for duty at Eisenhower's headquarters, and he never stopped singing their praises.

Early in 1943, WACs were assigned to General Mark Clark's Fifth Army. They moved with the troops advancing through Italy and were stationed just 6–12 miles from the fighting. These women lived in tents and tramped through rugged land just like the men. It quickly became apparent that the WAC uniforms were inadequate for the conditions of this mission. Eventually the women were allowed to wear men's clothing, but proper shoes still remained a problem.

At times throughout the war, more than 17,000 WACs were serving overseas.

Toughing It Out

The life of any soldier was tough, but women had additional problems. WACs serving in the Southwest Pacific suffered the most because of inadequate equipment and uniforms. The tropical heat and humidity proved the need for lightweight uniforms—which they didn't have. The women developed severe skin diseases and other illnesses because their heavy clothing never had a chance to dry.

Heat, humidity, and insects made life unpleasant. Mosquitoes carrying **malaria** were the biggest insect threat.

Mail deliveries to islands were infrequent, leaving many women without encouragement and support from loved ones for long periods of time. Recreational activities for women were also limited.

Despite the dangers and the difficulties, the women stayed and completed the jobs they were sent to do. By the end of World War II, more than 150,000 women had served in the WAC.

Production aides

Anchors Aweigh!

In July 1942, the WAVES (Women Accepted for Volunteer Emergency Service) was created by the navy. These women received the same military benefits and status granted to navy men. Approximately 86,000 WAVES served during World War II.

Unlike the WAC, decisions in the WAVES were made by a committee of women led by Mildred McAfee. This group fought for uniforms and training designed specifically for women.

WAVES In Training

The training centers for WAVES were held on college campuses. After one year at the University of Northern Iowa in Cedar Falls, boot camp was moved to Hunter College in New York. The courses were similar to those of the WAC, although WAVES did not have field training nor instruction in the use of weapons.

All recruits studied the nomenclature of their branch of the military, but the navy terms were especially interesting. Although most WAVES never worked on a ship, they learned the vocabulary that would prepare them for such an opportunity.

NAVY NOMENCLATURE

Civilian Word	Navy Term
wall	*bulkhead*
window	*porthole*
floor	*deck*
upstairs	*topside*
basement	*bottom deck*
stairs	*ladder*

Classroom rules were strict. The instructor referred to a WAVE by her last name only. A recruit was expected to stand at attention and call out her name before she spoke.

Recruits learned how and when to salute. The right hand should be pointed down and stiffened, with the thumb close to the forefinger. Then the sailor sweeps her hand up until the forefinger rests above the brow of her right eye. Any higher-ranking officer must be saluted.

For the most part, WAVES did not suffer unkind treatment from the men in the navy. The navy relationship was more like that of a brother taking care of his sisters.

A WAVE rotates the propeller of a training plane.

Job Training

After boot camp, additional training was held at various other college campuses. Officers' training was at Mount Holyoke and Smith Colleges in Massachusetts. Training at Oklahoma A&M, Indiana University, and the University of Wisconsin at Madison prepared WAVES for specific assignments. Although the curriculum was equal to two years of college, it was taught in five months of intensive class work.

Jobs carried out by WAVES were very similar to those of the WACs, including work on the Manhattan Project, preparation for D-Day, and decoding secret messages.

Typing on board a moving ship was a challenge. There were no computers, so typewriters were used. These typewriters had a movable carriage that held the paper against a black roller. The carriage moved as the typist hit the keys. At the end of each line, the carriage had to be shifted back to the next line.

When large ocean waves rocked the ship, the carriage rolled back and forth on its own. This caused the letter and number keys to jam.

Typists aboard ships also had to learn how to balance their weight on the chair. In choppy water, the chair could roll from one side of the office to the other.

WAVES Overseas

Many WAVES were frustrated by the law that prevented them from being assigned to duties overseas. In June of 1944, a request came from the naval operations in Hawaii. The war in the Pacific had been stepped up, and they needed to get men aboard ships. They asked for WAVES to fill the jobs onshore.

A new law was finally passed in Congress allowing WAVES to be stationed outside the **continental** United States. However, the women were restricted to Alaska, the West Indies, Panama, and Hawaii. They were also not allowed to be stationed near any combat situations.

On January 6, 1945, the first WAVES stepped ashore for duty in Hawaii. But by this time, the war was almost over, so Hawaii became the only place WAVES were ever stationed overseas.

The WASPs,
the SPARs, and the
Women Marines

The WASPs

Nearly 2,000 women served as pilots during World War II, in part due to Amelia Earhart's inspiration. Earhart was a female pilot who flew the first solo flights across both the Atlantic and Pacific Oceans. She proved that women pilots could be just as skilled as men. Even though she was lost at sea near the end of her record-setting, around-the-world flight, Earhart continued to be a role model for young women who wanted to become pilots.

Amelia Earhart

Nancy Harkness Love, a wealthy woman from Philadelphia, enjoyed piloting her own plane. She gathered a group of female pilots and formed a civilian ferrying, or delivery, service in September 1942. These experienced pilots flew planes from manufacturers to military bases. Love's group was called the Women's Auxiliary Ferrying Squadron (WAFS).

Jacqueline Cochran was a record-setting female pilot in the 1930s. She was also a close friend of Amelia Earhart. When the war started, Cochran spoke to Henry "Hap" Arnold, the chief of the Army Air Corps. She suggested a women's branch for the **corps**. With Arnold's blessing, Cochran created the Women's Flying Training Detachment (WFTD) in November 1942.

In August 1943, the WAFS and the WFTD merged into the WASP, or Women's Air Force Service Pilots. Cochran was in charge of the training. Love directed the ferrying branch of the organization. Recruits had to be at least 18 years old, have a pilot's license, and have logged several hundred hours of flight time.

Nancy Harkness Love

Jacqueline Cochran

31

Many of the jobs that WASPs performed were risky. The female pilots flew disabled planes to repair stations so they could be fixed. At times, they flew the targets for the men's **artillery** training. The women's planes would pull a wide, lengthy strip of material attached by a long steel cable. The success of a gunner's aim was determined by counting the holes in the material.

Some WASPs were test pilots. After they learned to fly new airplanes, they demonstrated the aircraft's abilities for the men.

Despite their skills and bravery, this new group of pilots still had no military status. They didn't receive insurance or other benefits like the male pilots in the Army Air Corps. Furthermore, the jobs these women did were considered too dangerous for any company to offer them regular health and life insurance. Thirty-eight women pilots died in the line of duty during World War II.

In January 1944, Congress was asked to make the WASPs part of the army, giving them military status like other women's branches. Confusion and rumors still surround the results of that vote. Some believe selfish ambitions or friction between officers caused problems. Others feel that General Arnold and Jackie Cochran were holding out for the creation of a whole new branch of the military—what later became the air force. Whatever the reason, the vote failed.

To add to their feelings of rejection, the WASPs received a letter from General Arnold in December 1944. The war was winding down, and he had been told to cut troops that weren't needed. He chose to **disband** the WASPS, claiming there were enough male pilots available at the time.

In addition, the ex-WASPs were unable to use their expertise in civilian life. Airlines did not hire women to fly passenger planes, and no one wanted to take lessons from a female pilot.

The SPARs

The U.S. Coast Guard opened its ranks to women recruits in November 1942. Dorothy Stratton was appointed director of the U.S. Coast Guard Women's Reserve. She knew the press liked to give the women's corps nicknames, so she suggested "SPARs," based on the Coast Guard's motto "**S**emper **P**aratus (**A**lways **R**eady)."

The Coast Guard's primary goal is to guard the U.S. coastlines. During World War II, German submarines were spotted on the East Coast, and rumors suggested that Japanese subs were lurking off the West Coast.

At first, SPARs were trained at WAVES centers. Officers then received further instruction at a Coast Guard academy. In 1943, the SPAR finally opened its own training center.

At this center in Palm Beach, Florida, most SPARs studied communications, including coding and decoding. SPARs also became radar and radio operators, in addition to duties similar to those of the other women in the armed forces.

During World War II, more than 10,000 women served as SPARs. Most were stationed in the continental United States, but in 1944, some served in Hawaii and Alaska.

The Women Marines

"Free a marine to fight!" a poster announced when the U.S. Marine Corps became the last branch of the military to accept women into their ranks. The leadership of the marines refused to allow nicknames, so the women were known only as "women marines." Ruth Streeter was appointed director.

The women marines' first boot camp was held at Hunter College with the WAVES. Afterward, a training center for women marines was established at Camp Lejeune in North Carolina.

Pride in the corps is very important to marines. Their reputation is based on dedication to hard work and high standards. The officers made sure the women marines were no different.

Three Marine Corps women at Camp Lejeune, North Carolina

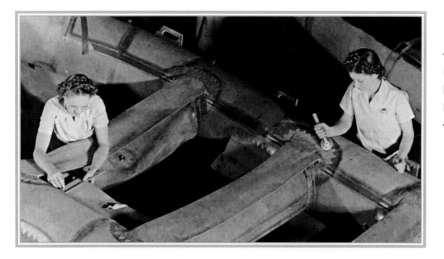

Women recruits were expected to undergo the same physical training as the men. Some women practiced parachuting from airplanes. Others trained to shoot cannons. However, no women actually made use of these skills during active combat in World War II.

Over 200 jobs were available to women marines. Some were mechanics, drivers, parachute riggers, and communications operators. Most worked at desk jobs in marine headquarters.

More than 23,000 women marines served in World War II. Generally they were restricted to duty in the continental United States, but near the end of the war, some were assigned to Hawaii or Alaska.

A marine sergeant practices
aerial photography.

In Harm's Way

Most branches of the military avoided placing women in danger. Only the WAC stationed women near combat, but they did it sparingly.

Some women in uniform were in harm's way by necessity. Army, navy, and Red Cross nurses worked near the fighting men and endured many of the same harsh conditions.

Pearl Harbor

Nurses stationed in Hawaii on December 7, 1941, knew something was wrong when they heard a terrifying mixture of sounds. Shortly before 8 a.m., the navy base was shaken by explosions and the deafening thunder of a skyful of low-flying planes. Black smoke boiled

Gas mask training

up from burning ships and buildings. Then the nurses recognized the red circles painted on the planes. Japan was attacking Pearl Harbor!

For about an hour and a half, the noise was constant. Diving airplanes dumped load after load of bombs. Explosions rattled the buildings. Fires roared and crackled. People cried out in pain and confusion.

Ten minutes after the attack began, the wounded started arriving at the hospital. As fast as they could, nurses treated their patients for terrible injuries and severe burns. Each time a bomb landed close to the hospital, the nurses shielded the injured and wished for a helmet or gas mask for themselves.

Circles of the Sun

The Japanese call their country Nippon or Nihon, which means "source of the sun." Their flag is white with a large red circle in the middle representing the sun. Red circles were painted on Japanese planes to identify them.

Europe and North Africa

Field hospitals are **portable** military medical units that move with fighting troops. When a field hospital moved to a new battleground, so did the nurses.

These women wore **fatigues**, boots, and helmets. A helmet was more than protection. It was a seat, a bowl for food, a laundry tub, and a sink for a quick cold-water bath. During the war, water for combat units was transported in large barrels on trucks.

Every time the troops moved, the hospital followed. The operating facilities had to be taken down and set up again. The nurses pitched their tents and dug foxholes nearby.

Foxholes were small ditches that were just large enough for one person. They were the only protection from attacks in the field. During an all-night raid, the nurses slept in their foxholes.

Anything with a red cross painted on it was considered off-limits to bombing. But the enemy often ignored the symbol. Some camps took a direct hit, and nurses were wounded or killed.

Some nurses got used to night raids. They were fascinated by the "gigantic Fourth of July celebrations." Flashes from **antiaircraft guns**, flares, and bursting bombs covered the sky.

Conditions for nurses were harsh, but these women felt strongly about the value of their mission.

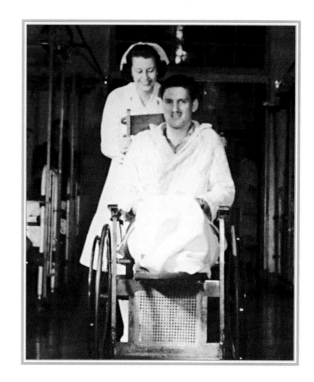

D-Day

Just days after the invasion of Normandy on June 6, 1944, the first nurses arrived in France. They waded ashore from small landing boats and walked across the same ground where the intense fighting had occurred a few days before.

The women saw tanks and trucks tilted at strange angles. Abandoned weapons and pieces of other military equipment were strewn about the beach. The land had been shattered by the battle.

The noise was constant. Planes thundered above them day and night. Antiaircraft guns clattered away. If a bomb landed nearby, **shrapnel** sprayed the tents, reminding the nurses of a hailstorm.

Field nurses were admired for their courage and dedication to their patients.

The Angels of Bataan

Army and navy nurses stationed in Manila, a major city in the Philippine Islands, felt lucky. Swaying palm trees and splashes of colorful flowers provided an island paradise for their tour of duty.

But less than 24 hours after bombing Pearl Harbor, the Japanese turned their gun sights on the Philippines. They began attacking on December 8, 1941, and continued to pound the islands for several days.

On January 1, 1942, the Allies were forced to retreat to Corregidor, an island in Manila Bay. It was called "The Rock." Under the rich **vegetation** that covered the mountainous surface, the Allies had built the Malinta Tunnel. It served as a hospital and a command center for General Douglas MacArthur.

Some troops were sent to the Bataan Peninsula across the bay. Bataan had two inactive volcanoes surrounded by dense jungle and swamps. This environment presented special problems.

The nurses were shocked when they were asked to set up another hospital in the few bamboo sheds and huts on Bataan. Their solution was an open-air hospital in the jungle.

The patients were placed on cots or padding on the ground. Their only shelter was the thick growth of jungle trees and vines.

Monkeys swung and chattered above. Lizards and huge rats scurried below. While making the rounds one night, a nurse bumped into a hanging cobra that her flashlight had missed. The swamp was a perfect home for mosquitoes that carried malaria to both patients and nurses.

In March, General MacArthur was reassigned to Australia. When he left Corregidor, he promised, "I shall return." General Jonathan Wainright was left in charge.

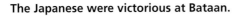

The Japanese were victorious at Bataan.

A month later, before the Japanese captured Bataan, the nurses stationed there were **evacuated** to the tunnel hospital on Corregidor. Many expressed regret about leaving their patients and the troops behind to face the possibility of torture by Japanese soldiers.

Prisoners of War

Corregidor fell to the Japanese in May of 1942. All of the Allied forces, including the nurses, were taken prisoner. They were sent to a Japanese prison camp for Allied civilians at Santo Tomas University in Manila.

At first the conditions were tolerable. For privacy, the prisoners built a village of shacks around the main building. Local **natives** were allowed to sell fresh fruits and vegetables to the captives.

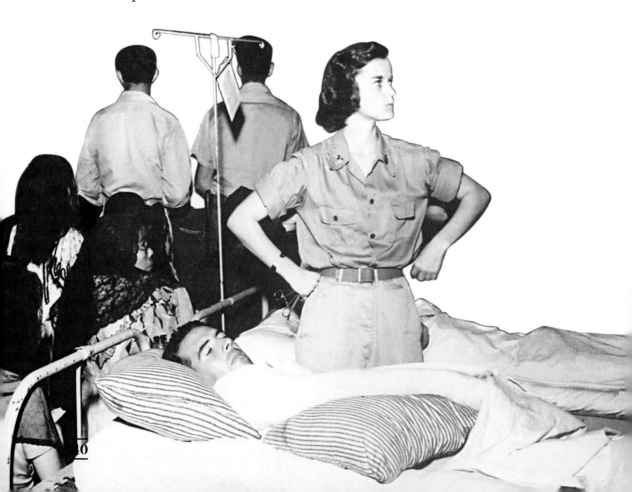

By 1944, the Allied troops were close to winning the war in Europe. Now they were able to focus on the Pacific front. Japanese soldiers took out their frustrations on the Allied prisoners held at Santo Tomas.

First they eliminated the supply of fresh fruits and vegetables. Then they stopped allowing any outside communication. Each day, the Japanese gave their prisoners less and less food. Most of what they did receive contained worms and bugs.

Death from starvation or disease was a daily occurrence. The nurses didn't have any medicines, but they still tried to save lives, even when they knew they couldn't. Work took their minds off their own hunger, but they continued to grow weaker every day. Any hopes for a rescue began to fade.

On Christmas Eve in 1944, American planes skimmed over Santo Tomas and dropped leaflets. The message read:

> The **commander in chief**, the officers, and the men of the American Forces of **Liberation** in the Pacific wish their **gallant** allies, the people of the Philippines, all the blessings of Christmas and the realization of their **fervent** hopes for the New Year.

It was the first real sign that a rescue was on the way. But when? How long could the prisoners hold on? Nearly three years had passed already.

Rescued!

One day in early February 1945, the prisoners heard machine guns in the distance and saw smoke from fires burning throughout Manila.

On the night of February 3, they heard a mechanical rumbling and the sound of gunfire just outside the walls of the prison camp. Searchlights flashed on the entrance to the camp.

With a grinding crunch of metal, an Allied tank plowed through the gate and rumbled over it. MacArthur had returned!

All 77 nurses survived the imprisonment, but many suffered long-term physical difficulties because of the ordeal.

V-E, V-J, and Beyond

"There was nothing but a dirt floor to dance on," said one nurse stationed in Germany. "But we had a good time anyway."

It was May 8, 1945. Germany had just surrendered, and the Allies were celebrating their victory in Europe (V-E Day).

Military people in the field noticed a lack of sound. No weapons were firing. Only a few quiet planes flew overhead. **Trenches** and **blackouts** were finally behind them. Home cooking and hot baths were just over the horizon.

A huge celebration took place in Times Square in New York City. Thousands of joyous people were jammed shoulder to shoulder. The crowd swayed like grain rippling in a field. Strangers were dancing, kissing, and hugging one another beneath a shower of streamers and paper thrown from the office windows above. People cheered and horns honked.

The same was true in New Orleans and other cities around the world.

Unfortunately, the celebrations were limited by the knowledge that World War II still wasn't over. The Japanese had not given up. Family and friends stationed in the Pacific were still in danger.

Then on August 15, 1945, after two atomic bombs, President Harry Truman finally announced that the war was over. Japan had surrendered.

Celebrations of V-J Day (Victory in Japan) were similar to those on V-E Day. These parties were even more spirited, though, since now the war was over. After the V-J Day celebrations, everyone was anxious for life to return to normal.

Going Backward

Many women found it difficult to go back to life as it had been before the war.

Military women were released from their obligations, and the corps were disbanded. All of a sudden, their new and exciting careers no longer existed.

Most people felt that women in the military had only been a successful "social experiment," an answer to an emergency need for more troops. Now that the war was over, women were no longer needed in the military.

Women on the home front also had to leave new jobs. During the war, they had successfully replaced men in various industries. But when the war was over, the men returned, and women were expected to go back to their traditional roles as mothers, teachers, and secretaries.

On the Home Front

The term *front* refers to an area in a war where fighting is going on. The people at home were fighting the war in their own way, so it became known as the "home front."

This attitude was a jolt to the women who were so proud of their accomplishments. They had proven to themselves and others that they were capable of doing whatever was asked of them. They had served their country in its time of need—where was the pride and respect they deserved?

After World War II, women began to organize and demand recognition for their abilities in both military and civilian life.

Moving Forward

After much debate and protest, Congress passed the Women's Armed Services Act in June of 1948. This act granted women a permanent place in the armed forces in times of war and peace.

Women pilots could enter the WAF, or the Women's Air Force. In 1947, the air force had been established as an independent branch of the military rather than part of the army as it had been before.

Today, women in the military still struggle for equality, but their courageous efforts during World War II were a giant leap in the movement toward recognition.

Captain Della H. Raney was the first African American nurse to report for duty in World War II.

Glossary

antiaircraft	designed to defend against attack by air
artillery	weapons
blackout	period of darkness used as a precaution against air attacks
blitzkrieg	war fought with great speed and force
branch	division of the military, such as the army, navy, marines, etc.
cavalry	army that travels by horseback
civilian	person who isn't in the military
close order drill	practice for marching in a close formation
combat	active fighting
commander in chief	president of the United States; an army's leader
continental	relating to a body of land that is all one mass; not including islands
corps	organized military group
cryptographer	person who deciphers, or figures out, secret codes
demerit	mark against a person's record for poor work or behavior
dictator	person who has complete control over a country
disband	to break up an organization

evacuated	forced to leave
fatigues	work uniforms worn by soldiers
fervent	with great emotion; showing strong feeling
field training	military training for combat conditions (see separate entry for *combat*)
front	area where battles take place
gallant	brave; courageous
Great Depression	period of low economic activity marked by high unemployment
inferior	less important than others
liberation	freedom
malaria	serious disease marked by chills and fever
master race	race of people thought to be superior (see separate entry for *superior*)
muster	gathering together of troops for evaluation and service
native	one who originally lived in an area
nomenclature	special vocabulary used for a branch of the military
paratrooper	soldier who drops into a battle area by parachute
patriotism	love and support of one's country
platoon	military unit, or group, of soldiers

portable	able to be taken down, moved, and set up again
quarters	place where a person lives or stays for a period of time
recruit	to sign up soldiers for the military; person who signs up for the military
rigger	person who prepares equipment for use
roll call	calling of a list of names to find out who is present
shrapnel	metal projectile that explodes in flight; pieces of such a projectile
superior	the best; more important than others
trench	long cut in the ground used for military defense
unit	group of soldiers
vaccination	shot given to protect against illnesses
vegetation	plant life that covers an area of land
veteran	person who was a member of the military

Index